# Grandmas & Grandpas

A book written
by grandchildren for
their grandparents
Edited by
Richard & Helen Exley

Published by Exley Publications Ltd.

*Other titles in this series:*
TO MUM
TO DAD
HAPPY FAMILIES
CATS (and other crazy cuddlies)
DOGS (and other funny furries)
A CHILD'S VIEW OF HAPPINESS
A CHILD'S VIEW OF CHRISTMAS
These titles may be ordered from your usual bookseller,
or send cheque/postal order to Exley Publications Ltd,
12 Ye Corner, Chalk Hill, Watford, Herts,
United Kingdom, WD1 4BS.
*(each £3.95 plus 50p postage)*

First published November 1975
Second impression July 1977
Third impression November 1977
Fourth impression February 1978
Fifth impression August 1978
Sixth impression August 1980
Seventh impression September 1980
Eighth impression November 1980
Ninth impression May 1981
Tenth impression August 1981
Eleventh impression August 1982
Twelfth impression September 1983

Designed by John Gorham/David Hillman
Front cover drawing by Alison Fogg, Age 8
Copyright © Exley Publications Ltd,
12 Ye Corner, Chalk Hill, Watford, Herts,
United Kingdom, WD1 4BS.
Printed in Hungary by Kossuth Printing House.
ISBN 0 905521 12 9

# Grandparents... fill in the gap that mothers and fathers leave out.

All the entries in this book are by real grandchildren, writing about grandmas and grandpas. They were sent in by children from eighty schools, scattered all over Britain, from Kinloss in Scotland to Sherborne in Dorset. The full list of schools appears on pages 63 and 64, and we are deeply indebted to the teachers and children who contributed.

The idea for the book had long been in our minds, but took shape through Helen's work as Editor of Help the Aged's newspaper YOURS, which goes to a million old people. She ran a 'What is a grandmother?' competition in YOURS, and was surprised how many of the entries came from children. These young people were so warm, so full of goodwill, that it seemed obvious that they should write the book.

We decided to collect more entries, and wrote to a number of schools around the country. In all, we had close on three thousand entries, and almost every entry could have gone in. A few were badly written, or went on about grumpy grans. But the overwhelming majority told a kind of love story;

each one presented a personal little cameo, each one told of a grandparent who was precious to that child.

We had the invidious task of selecting the well-written, the well-produced and the well-painted entries: sometimes just because they had a particular turn of phrase, sometimes because they were cute, sometimes because they were profoundly moving.

We were only sorry that we couldn't squeeze more into the book, because the grandparents would have been so proud to see what the children thought of them; it would have melted their hearts.

The things the children said in their letters confirmed our belief that there is a very special bond between grandchildren and grandparents: grandparents "fill in the gap that mothers and fathers leave out", as Carole Barrett of Norman Park School put it.

We already knew from our work for YOURS that this was true for older people. They describe in their letters the joy of a grandchild, of being able to touch and hold someone close again, perhaps years after a bereavement. People talk of a feeling of renewal in their lives, of a new meaning when a grandchild is born. And they discover that, if anything, the new grandchild is more precious even than their own firstborn. They now have time to enjoy the relationship, to get close to a child, and really to give.

And now these entries from the children give the other half of the story. They show that this love is returned in full. It isn't a one way thing.

At first the child doesn't seem to be aware of much more than the sweets and the presents. Many of the entries from the younger children make grandma seem like a walking tuck shop, a fount of goodies and Christmas presents. But very soon, especially amongst the girls, something else emerges. They begin to appreciate the time a grandparent has to give. Many of the letters talked of gran or nan as 'a best friend', somebody who you could talk to about your boyfriend, somebody you could say things to that you couldn't tell your parents.

It isn't that parents lack understanding; but within the family situation there may just be too many pressures. And in big classes at school, the teachers may not have much time either. Adults just don't seem to be there, ready to listen; and if a grandparent has managed to keep the channels of communication open, this is when they reap the reward of a close and lasting relationship.

Editing the book has been immensely enjoyable. It has proved, for us, that the relationship between the generations is alive and well. It's not dead, as sociologists would have us believe when they talk about the breakdown of the extended family and grandparents living in isolation.

In a way, this book is a way of saying thank you to grandparents; it's a way of saying thank you for all the plasters on sore knees, all those raspberry pies, all those patient readings of the 'Three Little Pigs', all the lessons, all the time so freely given. One little boy from Glebe House school in Hunstanton, Norfolk perhaps summed up the feeling of most of the entries when he wrote simply: "I send my love to grandparents, all over the world."

*Richard & Helen Exley*

# A grandma is old on the outside and young on the inside.

*John Wright Age 7½*

# Granpas are delightful things they date back to the last century.

*Simon Welch Age 10*

*Lynne*

# Grandmothers and Grandfathers give a home a friendly touch.

*Marco Orlandini Age 9*

Some of my night clothes as a baby were made from pre-Great War bottom-drawer petticoats. History for me is memories for them, yet they are not aged or dusty: Granny and Grandpa are real. A whole part of my childhood would be missing if I had not known them. With them I am at once a little girl and an object of pride and hope for the future.

*E J Slessenger*

Happy or sad I think that grandmothers are the wisest, most understanding people in the world (excluding of course grandfathers).

*Jane Moore*

# Definitions

You will never lose a Grandmother because you will usually find them on park benches or bingo halls.

*Gary Conway Age 9*

A Grandmother is a lady who either sleeps or knits.

*Sara Spurrier Age 12*

A Grandmother corrects your grammar and wipes immaginary dirt from your cheeks.

*K Phillips Age 11½*

Grandmothers are people who still do the spring cleaning.

*Maureen Dracey*

She's the person who tells me all the things about my parents, they would rather not have me know.

*Sarah Scott Age 15*

Most Grandparents have toilets and hard toilet paper.

*Michael Orloff Age 10½*

My Grandpa is tough outside, but soft hearted inside.

*Justin Birch Age 10*

Grandparents are cheerful, soppy things.

*Donna Pearce Age 12*

*Andrew Age 9*

The dictionary says, quite simply, a grandmother is "a father's or mother's mother" but had there been room, I'm sure they would have added...
Grandmothers are

Generous giving people
Regular churchgoers
Afternoon snoozers
Never (well, hardly ever) cross with you
Drinkers of whisky and water
Members of the Mothers' Union
Owners of "Minis"
Times crossword fanatics
Hospitable hostesses
Eaters of brocolli, spinach, cabbage and beans
Relaters of gossip
Scrabble players

and without Grandmothers, the world would be a different place.

*H. Bulley*

*Mark Marvis Age 9*

Your Granny loves you. No matter what you do.

*Paul Myers Age 10*

A Grandmother is kind and doesn't like half pences and other small change–she gives us them quite happily.

*Bobby Marston*

A Grandmother doesn't criticize.

*Anne Joplin Age 11½*

Gran's always have something up their sleeve like boiled sweets.

*Gemma Cummings Age 10*

Grandmothers wander around and look very suspicious. Grandmothers' bones are old.

*Caroline Curtis Age 11*

*Helen Alsop Age 8*

Justine Strachan. 7 yrs old
My Grandmother is my mammys
mother She is verey old and
nice as well and she brings
me nice things my Grandfather
is my mammys father a
Grandmother is a verey old
lady my mammy is my
Grandmother dauter and my
Grandfather dauter as well
She lives at 79 Chirton
Rd

*Justin Strachan Age 7*

11

My Granny is a knitting machine.

*Carolynn Shaw Age 7*

A Granny gives you a smoke of her fag in somewhere secret where your mum's not looking. A Granny is a very, very, very, very nice person. My Granny is my best Friend.

*Terry Worthington Age 9*

A Grandmother never tells us lies.

*James Denness Age 10*

# A GRAND MOTHER

*Simon Steer Age 11*

# Mostly sympathetic

A Grandmother is an elderly person who watches people walk past and hopes that someone will come and visit them.

*Simon Martindale Age 10*

My Great Grandad has a habit of buying me sweets and then eating them.

*Jay Coquillon Age 11*

When some grannies shake hands with you they put ten pence in your hand.

*David Shipton Age 9*

Grandmothers always come up with advice, which is given whether you need it or not.

*Rita Bourke*

A Grandmother is a little old lady, who comments on the weather and how tall you are getting, tells everyone the latest gossip and all about her son who came to see her. She lets you do what you shouldn't and if mum complains she says "Remember when you were little and I caught you dipping your finger in the sugar bowl? You're not too old for a clip round the ear".

*Jackie Thompson*

Grandmothers are the old in the world of the young, and are continually having the "good old days" wiped out of the conversation. They long to help and yearn to be loved.

*Rita Bourke*

A Granny is jolly and when she laughs a warmness spreads over you.

*J Hawksley Age 11*

Her shoes are all old fashioned now and her pantibloomers wow o wow.

*Sandra Fowler Age 9½*

## Appearance

# My Grandmother is crumpled.

*Richard Humphrey*

Some grandmothers are very small and some grandmothers are very big. You can get all different sized grandmothers really.

*Andrew Deboata Age 8*

The thing that makes grannies so jolly looking is the fact that as they get older they grow out instead of up.

*Jacqueline Hope*

My Grandmother is not very tall, but come to that she is not very short either.

*Sarah Green Age 10*

My Grandma is a little fat but Nowa-days most Grandmas are.

*Alan Richards Age 9*

My Grandma looks funny. She has got a long face and her chin wobbels when she walks.

*Michael Barbridge Age 7*

A grandmothers clothes remind me of a Princesses clothes, they are pretty and soft.

*Catherine Cardwell Age 9*

A grandmother can be tall or small but mine is midium and cuddly fat.

*Catherine Cardwell age 9*

Grandmothers are formal, strict, Victorian and covered in slippery black dresses tinkling with jet trinkets and smell of mothballs. My father's mother is a granny. She is comfortable and warm and soft, scented with eau-de-cologne and baking.

*E J Slessenger*

As you have proberly noticed my granny thinks time stands still and wears the same clothes as when she was small (except a few sizes bigger).

*Paul Milsom Age 10*

Grandmothers wear quite long coats to cover up their knobbly knees.

*Carol Stacey Age 7*

A Grandmother tells you to put on a coat or you will catch a cold. A Grandmother fusses over you. A Grandmother wears old fashioned clothes.

*Angela Mutch Age 11*

This is my grandma

Aligon

*Allison.*

Sandra Dale Age 9

# Habits

Grandmothers are rather a nuisance. They want everything so spick and span and tidy.

*Caroline Webb Age 10*

Grandmothers some times lock the door when they come out and when they get to the garden gate they go back to make sure they have.

*Eunice Hopkins Age 10*

Grandmothers are fat and put wigs on before they go to the door.

*Richard Dunmow Age 8*

My nanny has a good habbit of eating sweets every evening. I like this because I have some too.

*Nicholas Dunne Age 11*

My Gran has a habbit of naming things she calles her fridge Fredda and her two wirelesses big willy and little willy.

*Allison Anthony Age 10*

When my mum gets thirsty she has a cup of tea but when my nan gets thirsty she goes round to the pub.

*Jackie Holleley Age 10*

My Grandma has some very extraordinary habbitts.

*David Heys Age 10*

Perhaps the best definition of the grandmother, is somebody who spent her time telling your mother what not to do, when she was young. And now spends her time, criticism your mother for giving you the same advice.

*Calvin Giles Age 12*

My grandma knits all the time, though we have socks for more than 10 years.

*Anette Bromner Age 14*

It's nice to be Home

Jacqueline Hollely Age 10

(She's

She watches

ggle-box watcher)

Sandra Rendell Age 10

levision

## Colour Blocks

My grandmother is a box of
childrens building blocks
Each a different size and colour
Each one different from the other.

When I was young and cut my knee
She would become an enfolding, purple curve of
sympathy.

If I was caught doing, any wrong thing
She would be a rectangle, dark blue glowing.

If in dire need of help am I
She is a pulsating orange pillar,
That touches the sky.

When something special I have
Into a bouncing restless globe, she will go
Of a beautiful sunflower yellow.

To the dismal depths of depression I have been
So she has become a pyramid of gentle green.

When she is ill
And I make her jovial
A blazing turquoise star,
tells me I'm her cheering up pill.

Funny, and strange, how time should change.
Amazing how time should beg
I needed her once now she needs me.

*Quentin Radford Age 11*

# The nice thing about her, is that she says that I've got two homes, my home and their home.

*Julia Gambold Age 9*

*Brigid Cooper Age 7*

ndfather
n

*Emilio Esteban Age 10*

25

# Grandads

My Grandad can fix nearly everything.

*Helen Age 9*

Grandpa is usauly the grumpest of the pair. He is kind but not as kind as your gran.

*Elspeth Bridges*

Grandads are very lazy and sit back smoking and watch old films. Some grandads stay asleep all day until they feel hungry then they wake up. After tea they go back to sleep. My Grandad calls me bacon bonse.

*Mark Ward Age 9*

My Grandad is a funny sort of character because every time I go down to his house to borrow somthing for my Mum he says "No" and then lets me borrow it.

*Colin McRae Age 11*

My Grandad pretends he has a jelly tot tree.

*William Sholl Age 8*

Grandpas always have a bag of sweets in their pockets well as bits and bobs, such as a penknife, string, a compass, an animal bone and a toy soldier.

*Fiona Gibbings*

Grandfathers like cabbage and caulieflower and other awful things.

*Beth Age 10*

My Grandad is a safety shield against an angry mum.

*Rebecca Smith Age 11*

My grandpa used to rough and tumble with my brother But now both of them are past it.

*Richard Thompson Age 12*

# Inflation Inflation they say not like the good old days.

*Catherine Ashley Age 9*

*Andrew Barnett Age 10*

## My Grandparents.

I would like my Grandparents to be very loving, generous and thoughtful. I would like to be very kind in a way that they would care for me alot. I would like my Grandad to be rich enough to keep himself fit and well. He would live with my lovely old Granny out in the country-side, about a mile away from where I would live, so that I could visit them regularly. Their house and garden would be very neatly kept with lots of beautiful flowers which smell lovely. They both would be round about seventy years of age, but they still be quite well-off with alot of pension. My Granny would look after me well; she would be quite fussy about the way I dressed and cleaned myself. Also, she would always keep me looking tidy and smart. She would always wear funny colourful hats and clean colourful clothes. But she wouldnot ever wear lots of make-up or strong smelling purfumes.

They both would have very funny characters, they would be laughing all the time, and they would always say and do funny things. Granny always would try and tell me jokes, but she would always say them back-to-front, by mistake, then she would laugh. They would have very crazy habits. Whenever I would go around to their cottage, they always would be delighted to see me. They would sit me down, then make me drink a hot cup of coffee and then load me with chocolates and toffes. They would always know what I liked best. They would make me stay with them for as long as I could, and they would give me money to spend, without fail, every time I would go to their cottage. They would let me do what I wanted to in their enormous garden, which had stacks of things to do in it. Climbing trees, jumping walls, chasing rabits and lots of other exiting things. Somtimes Grandad would tell me stories of old-fashoned times. He would also play games with me which he would play when he was young. The two of them would never forget lots of presents for my birthday and for Christmas. They would always know what was right for me.

My Grandad would be short and stout, with a long curly mastchs, coloured grey-white. He would have a little bit of white curly hair, just around the sides. He would wear very smart looking clothes.

Geoffrey Baker    Aged 10 ys

# Grumbles

My Grandma is always saying don't touch, put that book away don't read in bed or something like that. She sayse put that car away. pick that up don't drew in that reading book. and at bedtime she even does it more. Go to sleep or you will be late for school in the morning, be quite, don't play with that, don't rip the blankets and then its brechfast time dreedfull don't lick your dish, clean your teeth wash your hands. I'm glad when I get to school and I don't hurry home. when I get home she starts again. did you get some stares yes Grandma. How many? Five. not good enough. and at bed time she starsts again.

*Dawn Age 7*

Gran Power is mum's mum. The only thing powerful about gran is the power behind her clouts, and I've had plenty in my time.

*Alinson Brice*

My nannys always chatting
My grandads a right misery
Between them
They make a right pair.

*Susan Nicoll Age 11*

My Fathers Mother is rather grumpy she likes to watch the news and moans to us when she hears about bombs as if we had planted them.

*Allison Anthony Age 10*

Graninies are awkward and they never want to do what other pepull are doing.

*David Hoggarth Age 9*

# Some people may think grandma's are special. I don't think grandma's are special they are just relations.

*Steven Alan Jones Age 8*

*Diane Barnett Age 7*

# Grannies used to be old with grey hair. But nowadays grannies can be quite young.

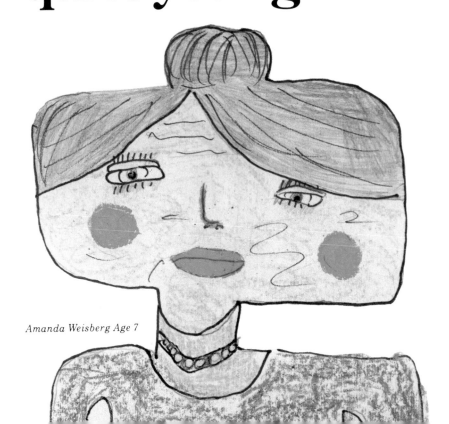

Amanda Weisberg Age 7

# About age

Grandmas say that the title makes them feel old–like a Grand piano, I suppose. As an alternative, how about Supermum?

*Isobel Blaber Age 14*

My Grandad looks very old to me and my brother.

*Trevor Cox*

My Grandparent's are both conciderate. They are both about the same age but that doesn't seem to bother them.

*Elizabeth Rose*

A Grandma is very nice and is some-time's old.

*Lynne J Gregory Age 9½*

My grandmother is getting older than she thinks.

*Clive Owen Age 10*

Grandpa is over 40 and under 90.

*Alexander Hambly Age 10*

Grannys always act young and seem young but are old.

*Lucy Deamer*

They aren't young, But my dad's catching up.

*N Arthur Age 13*

When they tell mom or dad Not to be silly I feel very, very young.

*Peter Wilson Age 12*

When she is sitting by herself she looks old and lonely. But when she has company she looks young again.

*Mary O'Gorman Age 11*

I Thought Dad was rather old – untill I met grandpa.

*Ian Laing Age 13*

Helen Brenchley    P. 6₂

## Granny

I was a granny in a play. It was about a boy wanting a puppy. I bought it for him at Christmas. Later on it was kicked out. It was meant to teach people not to buy animals that they couldn't keep. I had a shawl, an old walking stick and a pair of glasses on the end of my nose.

Grannies used to be old with grey hair. But nowadays grannies can be quite young. Grannies are very kind and loving. One of my grannies is in a wheel chair but she is very cheerful all the same.

*Helen Brenchley*

# A fascination with teeth

My Grandma has special toothpaste and pretending teeth.

*Clive Smith Age 7*

Once she lost her teeth later when I was running the bath they floated to the top. I think she is very typical.

*S Enright*

They often have a few false teeth Which in the morning are often found out Which lie besides the bed which are quite frightening They look like elephants fangs.

*Helen Turner*

If theres one thing that annoys me about gran is, she clicks her false teeth and she does it when theres any music going keeping in time with the tune.

*Alison Brice*

My Grand Mother is very unusual.
She has a very funny face.
Shes got gray hair and only four teeth left.
I fink gran should have two teeth out that will leave two.

*David Fitzgibbon Age 7*

My Grandma has false teeth I do not like the look of her when she's got them out.

*Richard Morrey Age 8*

I thing my Grand-dads great, he stayed with us all Christmas. My Grand-dad has no teeth and he hasn't got faulse teeth. When my Grand-dad laughs I can see the top of his gums and it makes me laugh to.

*Janette Wright*

My nanna hates false teeth. She is scared her dinner will get stuck underneath.

*Steven Whiskin Age 8*

'Ah blow it' shouted Grandpa and took out his false teeth and shook them at the driver who had just overtaken us. (Grandpa does not like being overtaken he hardly ever is though because he goes at such a speed). When we came up behind him, Grandpa waved his false teeth and shouted 'You crazy old fool'.

*D Farnworth*

24th January.

My Gran.
My Gran cannot sleep,
So she gets up very early.
When she goes upstairs
No one helps her or seems to care.
My gran wears false teeth
She takes them out then we have beef.

My Gran is very old
And is very, very bold
She is very kind
And for her age has a very good mind.

*Michael Croker Age 9*

# Food and cooking

She cooks delishush diners.

*Michael Barbridge Age 7*

Nans are people who give you fresh cream cakes and weak orange squash for tea and expects you to eat it all.

*Susan Garmston*

My grandmother makes lots of cakes, but the nicest thing about that is she lets me put the decorations on the top.

*Tanya Burch Age 9½*

Grandmothers fruit cakes are more fruit than cake mixture.

*Jane Hitchcock*

She makes real Yorkshire Pudding which has always risen about one quarter of an inch more than my mums.

*Sarah Richardson Age 10½*

My Grandmother is a good cook. Yock sherpuding is my best grub when I go to stay.

*Mark Harris Age 9*

A faint aroma of gingerbread and all good things mixed together, seems' to linger all around a grandmother.

*Elspeth Gordon Age 12*

A Grandmother by Rachel Williams

*Rachel Williams*

## Reginald

The best thing that I like about my Grandmother is, when she comes down in the morning and the fire's all lit she'll come and get dressed there. She'll stand by the fire and warm her bum and then my grandad will come along and he stands there looking at me and then he looks at Gran and he then gives a funny laugh, then creeps up to Gran and he rubs her fat tummy "Reginald" she shouts.
Her face then glows and wrinkles up and her eyes are full of laughter, her cheeks are a pair of roses and her glasses fall on to her nose.
"Reginald", she shouts, "if you don't stop that I'll have a burn't bum".

*Beverly Ward*

## Militant Grannies

They appear on the strikers camp,
                              with rolling pins
All armed to the teeth,
All ready to do battle with gnashing teeth,
One granny lets go with her Fiery left hook,
Which lands a TUC leader in the pond,
Where he floats on his back, like a dead duck,
They swing out left and right
With all their might,
And strike down every enemy in their sight,
And as the strikers Flee the scene.
Then the grannies take up the chase,
They swing their handbags like a mace
They smash them down, one by one,
And as each one Falls,
All the grannies let out their victory calls.

*Adrian John Bradley 12 years 9 mths*

*Sarah Woolston Age 9*

*Katy Osborne Age 8*

## Grandads

A grandad is a person you never forget, never.
I'm proud that he's my grandad.
And I'll never forget his hand in mine as we
walk down the street together.

*Suzanne Cairns Age 13*

I think my grandad is fantastic, most grandads
are. If you are saving up for something they are
like walking piggy banks and give you money.

*Jeremy Shilling*

I love the magic Grandad does, especially the
sweets he makes appear from my ear!

*Rebecca Smith Age 11*

Grandad grows lovely rasberries and always
pretends not to notice us eating them.

*Tracey Knight Age 8*

He cares for everything,
Everything,
But himself.

*Joanna Read Age 12*

My Grandfather always falls to sleep after the
football results are over, and he wakes up when
he hears his favourite word "food".

*Stephen Mouncher Age 11*

My grandfather is not really like any old man,
for he is 86 years old and has a special driving
license and swims in ice cold lakes in which I
would never dare to put my foot. One must not
think of him as a first class madman, or at least
one can think as one wants but I still think and
will think he is the nicest and most considerate
person I have had the chance to bump into.

*P Ham Age 13*

# A grandfather is somebody who outbalds Yul Brynner

*Un-named*

*Samantha Weinstein Age 9*

*Belinda Sacks Age 9*

# My Nanny and Grandad

Nanny...
...

...nys and Grandads are very kind to you.
...Sometimes they keep you talking when you're
...rush to leave. But they can't help it I suppose.
...ave two grandads and one nanny. My other nanny
...n heaven but she was always helping other people
...I know she is a very special angel.

*Sharon Watson Age 9*

# Some people aren't lucky enough to have a Nanna so they have to hire one.

*Anne Galbraith Age 9*

I have worked out that the youngest a legal grandmother can be is thirty three and three quarters. This is not often the case. Normally they are in their late fifties or early sixties. To a young child, this seems ancient, but as they grow up, and see their parents pushing the forties, they realise how young they really are!
I always associate grandmothers with knitting and darning—very useful when you go through your socks at the rate I do! They are often widows and therefore have to be visited fairly often.
If they drive, they are highly lethal–either driving too slowly or in the middle of the road (or both!)
If and when they send you postcards from Eastbourne or Ramsgate (where they go and visit great aunty Flo) their writing is always thin, wobbly, spidery and totally illegible. They feel the cold far too easily, require an electric blanket, a

thick vest, wooly draws and the central heating on in the middle of summer!

Their cutlery is normally silver (whether they can afford it or not) and the table cloths and napkins are always stiffly starched.

They love potted plants, Radio 4 BBC 2 and old china ware. They have an annoying habit of never having their 'spectacles' handy when they need them.

One big problem they all have in common is being very deaf. This means that everyone has to speak slowly and loudly for them to hear. When given a deaf aid for a Christmas present they complain when you speak too loud!

At meal times even though they eat very little, they feel obliged to leave something (an old victorian habit I believe) which is very annoying indeed.

On the whole despite their annoying ways, I like grandmothers very much, knowing that someday I'll probably end up like them!

*L Horne Age 13*

*Linda McLaughlin Age 9*

49

# All the time in the world

She has a part of her own and a future which belongs to everyone. She leads an empty life of her own which is filled by the lives of others. Most of all she is a person who will always have time to see you when the rest of the world is busy.

*Gill Webb*

Grandmas are always slow but they do not mind for they have all the time in the world.

*Malcolm Andrew Age 10*

Grandmas have nothing to do
But talk to you.

*Catherine Mellors*

Grannys are dearly loved by every-one. When your mother tells you you are going to spend a day or two at your granny's you can't wait. When you fall over and cut yourself mummy and daddy are always too busy to put a plaster on. So the only person who is not too busy is granny. At night time granny's tuck you up in bed and make you nice and snug.

*Jane Hibbs Age 9*

A Grandmother is a person who will never get tired of your chatter however long you go on for.

*Julia Macdonald-Smith Age 12*

I personally believe that grandmas would knit to the end of the world!

*Simon W. Debenham Age 11.*

My Grandmother is very patient. She would have to be with me around!

*Helena Leeson Age 10*

Grandparents live in their own funny world where time seems To go backwards.

*Kevin J Brown Age 12*

Paul Yeowell Age 10

# Bribery

Grandmas usually take off their glasses to find their purses, and, as most grandmas were born in the times when a penny was as big as a twopence bit, you often get twenty pence instead.

*Simon W. Debenham Age 11*

Grannies are very necessary for letting you do things you are not allowed to do generally, like watching "The Late Night Horror Movie" or eating too many sweets than are good for you, or not making you eat a nasty pudding.

*Kate Clancy Age 14*

My nanna lets me lick the cake mixture when she is finished. She lets me leave my food, and she spoils me so much that when I grow up I won't want anything.

*Sandra Webb Age 10*

Most grandmothers will spoil you if they can, but parents will butt in just as you're about to eat your third helping of cake, it's most annoying.

*Helen Schwendener Age 11*

The 'grandmother' is usually a great source of the children's income as she nearly always gives them perhaps 50p after a happy but exhausting visit. The money is usually for all her grand-children ("little angels"). They usually stick their hands out suggestively or start snivelling that they can't afford a teddy bear or a skiing trip to Aviemore.

*Charles Robert Fenwick Linfoot Age 13*

Every time I went over to her flat I got 20 or 25 pence. As I liked my grandmother I went over to her flat about five times a week.

*Andrew Austin Age 10*

Mum says you're spoiling us but do they listen oh no. Presents here presents there presents everywhere. I like Grandmothers spoiling me.
Darlings they always say, while mum thinks what rubbish.

*Catherine Ashley Age 9*

One of a grandmother's most prized privileges is to spoil her grandchildren. She arrives armed with pockets full of sweets, and special pocket-money to buy the child the things denied it by its parents for numerous good reasons—no cream cakes because they are too rich, for example. Granny stuffs the child full of sweets and cakes, and then leaves before it is sick.

*Tessa Ing*

When my mum tells me to do something I do not want to do I tell my Grandmother and she talks my mum out of it.

*Sonia Allan Age 10*

My nanna lets us stay up and watch horror films. My nanna is really really really nice.

*Mark Robinson Age 9*

*Colin Fleetham Age 11*

### This is my Grandmother

Her frail body carries her along
Slowly but surely she crosses the road
It seems miles long
As she makes sure of her steps.
This is my grandmother
The kindest of her kind.
Looking back I remember the things she did for us.
When we were young we stayed with her
We had fun together
The walks, the talks, the games
When we were ill she spent a lot of time looking
after us
Even when there were things to be done
We were her sole concern always.
Now we look after her.
Talk to her and look after her with her ills
We try to pay her back for her kindness to us
But it would take forever.

*Susan Punter*

### Who can measure Grandmothers?

She seemed in a mask or costume
As much as a hat or glove.
For in her talk was youth and life
As pure as a beautiful dove.

Her mask was of wrinkled skin
Attached onto her face.
It was not really her because it did not fit
It belonged to another time and place.
But the more she talked and as I watched her
She shed the mask from her face.

A light as new as spring shone in her eyes
And in her movements a youthful grace.

Age is but a word of time
A thing which we created.
A thing which is measured like the pips on a radio.
But who can measure grandmothers
And put them into hours and minutes
Of knowledge kindness love and care?

The nearest measurement there is for me
Is that They are like the jewels in a watch
The watch is the world
And the wheels are the tools of the spring
The spring is life
The more jewels the better the watch.
My Grandmother is not diagem or paste
But a clear and sparkling diamond.

### A Grandmother

This small grey woman, a mother grown old,
By her hair and her wrinkles her age can be told,
Her past is a dream, an impossible hope,
For her children are married now and able to cope.
Her role as a mother has vanished and gone,
As the moon loses its role when up comes the sun.

But the birth of a Grandchild means new life has
begun,
The birth of a Grandmother, Parents and son.
Now there is a role, a part to be played
For this small grey woman, a grandmother is
made.
New qualities of joy have begun to show
Is this the same woman whom I used to know?

She now is a grandmother, a person who shares
A person who loves and a person who cares,
Her face has an expression of understanding and
love,
Of normal standards she towers above.
Her time to all is so generously given,
A person who I'm sure is destined for heaven.

*Sally Lloyd Jones Age 14*

*Dawn Mallard*

My Grandmother is a refuge. She is a gentle 'relic' of the past (although I don't thing she would like me calling her that). She is part of the past it is nice to think she has travelled through the years and is still so sensible and kind.
They take care of us, in loving us, but ask for nothing in return.

*Susan Philpot*

*Tracy Chennells Age 9*

### *How can she make them understand?*

She sits there living,
In her memories,
The young men, the laughter
The river boats,
Summer teas and romance,
Romance unlike any other,
Special, strong and
Everlasting.

Nothing is left now,
Only memories,
Though life goes on, but
She cannot understand
Remembering her long quiet childhood,
Which no longer remains,
Life was simple,
And days were long and happy
Children now are so restless
And unloving, taking everything
For granted, awaiting their maturity
Wasting their long, lazy days
Of innocence
Oh, how can she make them understand?

*Susan Legg Age 15*

*Diane Barnett Age 7*

58

## A Refuge

When you go to her with your pride bruised
and hurt; she never takes sides, but helps you to
think fairly and to see the other person's point of
view. She knows the problems that all the .
members of her family go through, and is able,
from her own experience to give advice.
She is usually a sympathetic listener–to what
must seem to her, your personal inconsequential
(compared with some of the ones that she has to
face during her life-time) problems. She never
tries to advise her children on grand-children,
unless she is asked to do so, and lives her own
life, far enough away, so as not to be a nuisance,
but close enough (to her children) to be a help in a
crisis. In short a grandmother is a refuge.

*Amanda Evans*

## Nana

Nana tells tales that she told to mother when
she was a child. Many stories of exciting
adventures that happened a long time ago. They
did not have the luxuries that we have, but
dancing the Lancers in their large living room
when the furniture was pushed aside, singing
round the piano, telling stories by the blazing fire
whilst they ate hot muffins. Skating on the frozen
park lake in the winter, riding on the top of an
open deck tram car, all these more than make up
for television and holidays abroad. I hope my Nana
will stay with me for a long time, and when I have
the farm I long for, she will be able to live with
me and feed the chickens. We will have a blazing
log fire and she will tell us stories of the past.

*Dawn Williams Age 10*

# Love

I would not want my nanny to go up to heaven.
*Michael Orloff*

My Grandmother is not plump but nice and comfortable, when she cuddles you, you can nestle down and feel safe and secure.
*Angela Dobson Age 10*

Our granny is not very old
I don't mind how old she is.
I would not want another gran because ours is the nicest one.
I wouldn't swop her for under or over half a crown.
*Jane Clarke Age 10*

My nanny is in heaven but she was always helping other people so I know she is a very special angel.
*Sharon Watson Age 9*

Grandmothers are very useful for showing you how to do lots of different stitches.
*Caroline Webb*

If I have a secret I will always tell Grandmother not anyone else.
*Joanna Simmonds Age 8*

You can tell them secrets of all the bad things you have done and they won't tell our mothers. Then they tell you about all the wicked things they did when they were little.

If we get bored with our Mum and Dad telling us what to do, there's always someone waiting for us with her arms out.
*Helen Tidy Age 9*

A grandmother is someone you love helping.
*Jane Farrell Age 11*

# A Grandmother is a mother who has a second chance.

*Caroline Flitcroft Age 11*

*Kim Curd Age 11*

*Julian Humphrey Age 10*

# This book was written and illustrated by the children from these schools.

Arnold Coppice Junior School, Nottingham.
Aston Fields County School, Bromsgrove, Worcs.
Ainsdale Church of England School, Merseyside.
Abingdon School, Abingdon, Berks.
All Saints Church of England School, Fulham, S.W.6.
Allithwaite Church of England Primary School, Grange over Sands, Cumbria.
Allington School, Allington, Lincs.
Bishop Harland Church of England Primary School, Sunderland.
Bedales School, Petersfield, Hants.
Burton Road School, Barnsley, Yorks.
Benenden School, Cranbrook, Kent.
Bishop Fox's Girls' School, Taunton, Somerset.
The Boys' High School, Colchester, Essex.
The Beacon School, Salisbury, Wilts.
Cassiobury Junior Modern School, Watford, Herts.
Cullercoats Junior School, North Shields, Northumberland.
Claremont County Primary School, Tunbridge Wells, Kent.
Canford Heath Middle School, Poole, Dorset.
Chipperfield Junior Modern Infant School, Chipperfield, Herts.
Chipping Ongar County Junior School, Ongar, Essex.
Downsbrook Upper School, Worthing, Sussex.
Downsbrook Lower School, Worthing, Sussex.
Deanwood County Junior School, Gillingham, Kent.
Elton County Junior School, Bury, Lancs.
Ellington County Junior School, Maidenhead, Berks.
Eastbourne High School, Eastbourne, Sussex.
Fairfield County Junior School, Widnes, Lancs.
Finchingfield Primary School, Braintree, Essex.
Fort Primary School, Leith, Edinburgh.
Grove County Primary School, Trowbridge, Wilts.
Godolphin School, Salisbury, Wilts.
Glebe House School, Hunstanton, Norfolk.
Hill House Prep. School, Doncaster, Yorks.
Heatherside County Junior School, Fleet, Hants.
Hawnes School, Haynes, Bedford.
Iford & Kingston School, Kingston, Nr. Lewes.
Juniper Green Primary School, Edinburgh.
Kinloss Primary School, Kinloss, By Forres.
Kings of Wessex Secondary School, Cheddar, Somerset.
Leighton County Primary School, Montgomery.

Melborn County Primary School, Royston, Cambs.
Normand Park Junior Modern School, London S.W.6.
Newland High School, Hull, Yorks.
Our Lady of Compassion R.C. Junior School, Formby, Liverpool.
Parkside Primary, Jedburgh, Roxburgh.
Preston Park Junior School, Wembley, Middlesex.
Pinner Park Middle School, Harrow, Middlesex.
Pitcorthie School, Dunfermline, Fife.
Pyrford County Junior School, Woking.
Putney High School, London S.W.15.
Queens Road County Primary School, Cheadle Hulme, Cheshire.
Rothwell County Junior School, Rothwell, Northants.
Red House School, Stockton on Tees, Teesside.
Rayleigh County Junior School, Rayleigh, Essex.
Rough Close C.E.P., Stoke on Trent.
R. A. Butler Junior School, Saffron Walden, Essex.
Sacred Heart Junior School, Hammersmith.
Suckley Primary School, Suckley, Worcs.
Silkstone Primary School, Barnsley, Yorks.
St. Helen's School, Northwood, Middlesex.
Stanburn Middle School, Stanmore, Harrow.
Simon Langton Grammar School for Boys, Canterbury, Kent.
St. Giles Junior Modern, Pontefract, Yorks.
Sears Green County Primary, Northfleet, Kent.
Sutton High School for Girls, Sutton, Surrey.
Sherbourne School for Girls, Sherbourne, Dorset.
St. Lawrence College, Ramsgate, Kent.
Southend on Sea High School for Girls, Southend on Sea.
Swithun Wells R.C. School, Chandlers Ford, Hants.
St. James C. of E. School, Chipping Campden, Glos.
Stowe School, Buckingham, Bucks.
Scaltback Middle School, Newmarket, Suffolk.
Tavistock C.P. School, Devon.
Trinity Road County Junior School, Chelmsford, Essex.
Ulpha C.E. School, Broughton in Furness.
Ulverston Victoria High School, Cumbria.
Woodstock C.E. Primary School, Woodstock, Oxon.
Wellington High School, Telford, Shropshire.
Walton County Primary School, Walton on Naze, Essex.
Watford Grammar School for Girls, Watford.